100 AMAZING BUSINESSES YOU CAN START WITH 100 DOLLARS

Dr Kenton Edward Emmanuel Connor

Table of Content

INTRODUCTION: Starting Up a Viable Business with $100

Have you at any point longed for a business of your own? What's keeping you down?

If the appropriate response isn't having enough cash to begin, at that point, this eBook will help unravel business ideas and ventures you can start with less than $100.

A lot people engage in random temp jobs to take care of numerous bills, despite the skills they have garnered so far, people still need jobs that can serve as a viable, profitable side hustle that can pump in the cash.

However, for some aspiring entrepreneurs, raising a substantial capital to start up a business venture might prove tricky. This eBook is targeted at entrepreneurs seeking great business ideas they can venture in with capital as low as $100!

So, let's get into it! Let's take you to a world of business ideas you can start with less than $100. Here is a well-researched list of 99 great businesses you can start-up with $100 or less!

1. **Tutoring:**

   There are a great deal of students who need help with each subject, going from inception to college. If you have this kind of knowledge, at this point you need to begin your own coaching services which can be an engaging business that requires basically no capital.

The students as of now have their learning materials with them so they'll be no need to spend funds.

2. **Adult Companion:**

2016 records an excess of 49 million individuals in the U.S. aged 65 years or more who were alone. That figure is seen to be developing **FOR** around 98 million in 2060. That implies that there are a handful of **AGING** persons who are searching for somebody to stay with them or families searching for exhortation on the most proficient method to care for their friends and family.

3. **Freelancing:**

Regardless of whether you're a writer or web designer, freelancing can be a worthwhile business that essentially requires just your ability, PC and internet connection. With the availability of various sites that post freelance gigs, you ought to have no issue beginning.

4. **VLOGGING:**

   Since each PC, tablet, and cell phone **COME** outfitted with an inherent camera, anybody can begin making recordings and presenting them on YouTube. In the event that you have **THE INFORMATION** you need to share, or are simply staggeringly alluring, you can then profit from your video blog through ads.

5. **Menu Planning:**

   A lot of individuals are ambivalent with regards to their food. That is the reason they're willing to employ somebody to assist them with arranging out their dinners. This is a minimal effort idea for any individual who appreciates working with food yet doesn't have the resources to get ready and serve it.

6. **Handyman:**

   In case you're ready to make minor family unit fixes, such as changing out a broken electrical outlet or fixing a channel under the kitchen sink, at this point you can start a business with this because it is another sought after business that doesn't cost a lot to dispatch. You could even consider starting on TaskRabbit, a commercial center stage for little occupations.

7. Managing Web Design:

There are endless websites out there that instruct you on the fundamental website composition. Get familiar with other expertise today. Regardless of whether you aren't a website specialist, you could discover a designer that charges moderately and still gives you a proficient website composition firms. The key here is dealing with the procedure - most businesses would prefer not to do this and are happy to pay.

8. Sharing Economy Rental:

With the "sharing economy," an ever increasing number of individuals are selecting to lease things rather than buying them. You can lease things ranging from your parking spot to your furnishings. Start-up a niche and gradually stir your way up. For instance, you could begin leasing yard gear like rakes, scoops or leaf blowers. In the event that you don't effectively possess them, you can buy them for under $100.

9. **House/Pet Sitter:**

This thought basically requires no underlying venture. You can begin asking your family, companions and neighbours if they need somebody to watch their home or pet when they leave town.

10. **Lawn Care:**

In the event that you have a green thumb, and you appreciate being outside and have the apparatuses to begin - like a lawnmower, weed-whacker or cutting tool - at this point, this is an easy decision to start a business. The main fundamental expense is publicizing and promoting your business.

11. **Secretarial Administrations:**

There are a great deal of private companies and people who need administrations like composing, translating and editing. For whatever length of time that you have a PC, a printer and the important abilities, your business ought to be a great idea to go.

12. Project Management:

In all honesty, not all organizations have an in-house venture director, which implies that activities can rapidly get off course. Organizations are frequently ready to enlist outside undertaking administrators to keep their groups centred.

13. Homemade Gourmet Nourishment:

Regardless of whether its soup blends, jams or chocolates, individuals love gourmet nourishment items. What's more, since you most likely have a kitchen, you simply need cooking supplies, branding and fundamental marketing materials to begin.

14. Proficient coordinator:

We sure do live in a very materialistic world, and it's anything but difficult to begin getting overpowered by all the stuff that is expanding our homes. Simply take a look at the rising ubiquity of Marie Kondo. Proficient coordinators can assist individuals with recovering their homes for close to $20 or on characterized advertisements.

15. **Cleaning Services:**

Cleaning administrations are very common. You can stand apart from the opposition by offering a green cleaning administration that utilizes eco-accommodating and regular items. You may even have the option to make some of them yourself and sell them for additional money.

16. **Grocery Conveyance:**

Some significant markets offer conveyance administrations, yet not every one of them does. There's an opportunity your neighbourhood store doesn't, either. That is the point at which you can charge clients to have you go to the store for them and afterward convey staple goods to their homes.

17. Individual Attendant:

An individual attendant deals with everything from taking customers to the air terminal, carrying the canine to the vet or overseeing plans. It's basically being somebody's very own associate.

18. Creating Information Items:

If you have an exposure in a particular specialty, at this point, you can begin selling your insight by making items like eBooks or instructional recordings. The expense is generally your time, domain name and web hosting.

19. Blogging:

If you're acquainted with a particular niche, at that point you can dispatch a blog where you share your insight. You can gain cash by selling advertisement space, becoming an affiliate or beginning a subscription administration.

20. **Window Cleaning:**

Window-cleaning is numerous individuals' least most loved family task, and a window-cleaning administration doesn't require a lot of funding to get profitable.

21. **Interior Creator:**

Usually, mortgage holders and entrepreneurs are searching for individuals to plan comfortable, sorted out and beneficial spaces.

22. **Flier Dispersion:**

Neighbourhood organizations despite everything recruit individual services to give out flyers or place them under windshield wipers. You basically simply need to make a ton of duplicates, and that is not a significant speculation.

23. **Programming:**

Figuring out how to program or code, for example, with the article situated unique programming language known as Ruby, is one of the most rewarding business out there.

24. Virtual Assistant:

This activity is like being an individual partner - noting calls, reacting to messages and keeping your customer's calendar. The difference is that, you can do this remotely.

25. Social Media Advisor:

Organizations and people are consistently watching out for individuals to oversee and keep up their social channels for them, and numerous organizations will pay $500 or progressively a month for these administrations.

26. Catering:

If you're a remarkable cook, however would prefer not to put resources into an eatery, at that point you can begin your own catering business legitimately from your own kitchen.

27. Mobile Fixing:

Need to put your own mobile repair administration? Start one that includes you, heading off to the customer. Regardless of whether if it's fixing a cell phone, a PC or a household item, this idea doesn't require in excess of a vehicle, promoting and your own ability.

28. Resume-Composing Administration:

Many individuals experience issues composing astounding resumes and that may make them miss out on an occupation they've been looking for. In the event that you have skill for forming resumes, it can turn into a gainful business.

29. Occasion Decorator:

Everybody needs their home or office to look happy for an up and coming occasion, however not every person can get that going. In the event that you can pull off that seasonal joy, at that point this is another business that doesn't require a lot of capital.

30. **Domain name-purchasing:**

You can purchase a domain for next to nothing - some of the time for under $1. In the event that a business tags along and needs that space, here and there they'll be eager to pay as much as possible for it.

31. **Flipping Sites:**

Utilizing a webpage like Flippa, you can buy a site, develop it and sell it. You can transform this into a worthwhile business.

32. **Cleaning Dryer Pipes:** Dryers get stuck with build up, and if an excess develops, you could have a house fire on your hands. Since this is a territory that is regularly ignored, you can begin a dryer conduit cleaning business with only a vacuum and some essential showcasing.

33. **Affiliate Advertizing:**

If you have a blog or page with a lot of followers, at this point you can become an affiliate. Basically, this implies that at whatever point you prescribe an individuals' items or administrations, you can utilize your own extraordinary affiliate interface that you've mentioned from the organization (or a commercial center like Amazon). At whatever point a guest taps on that connection and makes a buy, you'll get a commission.

34. **Dropshipping:**

Dropshipping is selling items for organizations on destinations like eBay. At whatever point the item is sold, the organization handles everything else, for example, delivering and you get paid for selling the products.

35. **Snow Expulsion:** if you have snow scoops and possibly a furrow, at that point this business idea can make you genuine money. Nonetheless, it's totally reliant on the climate.

36. **Pet Nurturing:**

Imagine being a pet lover and you appreciate being around pets and can wash them, trim their nails and give them a better than average hair style, at this point, this can be a genuine cash producer without a lot of a venture.

37. Pooper Scooper:

It's certainly not the most fabulous occupation, yet you'd accomplish something that a great many people fear so much that they'd pay another person to do it for them.

38. Occasion or Gathering Organizer:

If you're sorted out and an organizer, at that point dealing with the courses of action for birthday events, retirements or weddings can be a beneficial business.

39. PC Fix and Upkeep Supplier:

Think about all the PCs out there that crash or need refreshing. Do you believe that every owners of Pc has the specialized information to deal with any trouble shooting issues? Think about beginning your own business.

40. Holistic Mentor or Guide:

Numerous individuals recruit mentors or guides to assist them with things like shedding weights or discovering purpose, satisfaction and happiness.

41. Accountant:

It's significant for organizations and people to keep their records perfect and clean, however, not every one of them has the opportunity to do as such. That is the point at which they employ somebody to maintain their books in control for them.

42. Tax Arrangement:

Getting ready assessments is another need, yet the majority of us don't have the opportunity or information to deal with this errand. In case you're knowledgeable on the most recent expense guidelines and appreciate doing the math, this can be a worthwhile business during charge season.

43. Book Composing:

Did you realize that both Amazon and Apple have book-distributing arms? Regardless of whether you compose an instructional book, cookbook or science fiction experience, you would now be able to distribute it at basically no expense.

44. Decking Business:

Introducing your own deck may sound simple, however, it can get dubious. That is the point at which you can make all the difference by introducing floors for other people. The best part is that you don't have to stress over stock - you'd just be concentrated on installation.

45. Painting Addresses on Curbs:

Numerous office and private clients would readily pay you to shower paint their location on the check. You'd simply need some splash paint and a location unit to begin.

46. Parking Garage Striping:

There are a lot of parking garages that need new stripes. You can begin with a straightedge instrument and shower paint. As you win more cash, you can buy proficient gear.

47. Business Planning:

On the off chance that you've just made an effective business, at this point you can really transform that information and experience into another business. New entrepreneurs will pay for somebody to help direct them in building up their own effective marketable strategy.

48. Homemade Natural Cleansers and Beautifying Items:

Selling regular and natural items is a flourishing business. Regardless of whether you don't feel good in creating your own common cleansers and beauty items, you can outsource for organizations that do.

49. Logo Structure:

If you're an imaginative and individual, at that point planning logos is a generally simple business to begin. You can do anything from planning extraordinary logos to modifying thoughts from layouts.

50. Interpreter:

Organizations urgently need people who can communicate in the language of whatever market they're entering

51. Re-Establish/Up-Cycle Furniture:

If you're smart to easily detect a pre-owned household item that needs some TLC, you could make the fixes and exchange. That is practically all benefit.

52. eBay Dealer:

Individuals have been living for a considerable length of time selling of old garbage on ebay, exchanging things and outsourcing.

53. Application Designer:

With the portable transformation going full speed ahead, the interest for applications has never been higher. Regardless of whether you don't have programming aptitudes, you can even now enlist somebody to make your application a reality.

54. Individual Gourmet Specialist:

In contrast to providing food, which may just keep you occupied two or three days out of each week, individual gourmet specialists are liable for preparing breakfast, lunch as well as supper for customers.

In any case, you can invest, the greater part of your energy planning supper that simply should be warmed. That permits you to take on more customers.

55. Fitness Coach:

Despite the fact that wellbeing is a need for the greater part of us, it very well may be challenged to remain on target as well as ensure that you practice accurately without harming yourself. By turning into a fitness coach, you can spur and screen individuals while they work out.

56. Embellish Items:

On the off chance that you don't have the devices or abilities to assemble things, you can generally adjust from the scratch or improve a current item.

Take mosquito nets, for instance - they're insipid, however you could beautify them with strip or globules to make a one of a kind item.

57. Photographer:

There's constantly an interest for photographers at exceptional occasions like weddings, birthdays, funerals, dedications etc. You can take up a skill which can be lucrative.

58. Flea Market Distributing:

Flea markets are as yet flourishing, and you can for the most part lease a spot for the day for just $20. You can sell anything from the garbage laying around your home to the produce you developed in your lawn to carefully assemble crafts.

In numerous territories, there are various flea markets occurring all through some random week, so this can without much of a stretch become a continuous gig.

59. Online Content Developer:

Organizations need bunches of content today. If for instance, they don't have an in-house group to make and produce content, they frequently employ capable outside persons to do it for them.

60. Website Designer:

Everybody wants to have a site nowadays, especially for the growth or publicity of their businesses and for the individuals who don't have the opportunity or information; you can build up their site for them.

61. Selling Plants on the Web:

On the off chance that you have a green thumb and the space, at this point you can sell plants on the web. It's really a developing specialty since individuals are getting progressively worried about where their plants began from, and you can likely charge less the huge box stores.

62. Calligrapher:

If you have better and an outstanding handwriting, at this point, you can charge individuals to make transcribed solicitations.

63. Selling Crafts:

If you can really make high quality artworks, similar to adornments and furniture, at this point you can sell those items on destinations like Etsy.

64. **Home Childcare:**

You'll unquestionably need to get the best possible licenses and permits, yet this is a business that you can begin at home.

In certain territories, childcare costs around $15 60 minutes, so this can be a worthwhile business.

65. **Clearing Out Abandoned Homes:**

At whatever point a bank abandons a home, they need to enlist somebody to wipe the spot out.

If it's all the same to you getting somewhat messy, you needn't bother with a lot to begin this sort of business.

66. **Reusing Scrap Metal:**

A few people drive around and take garbage, for example, broken dryers, off of individuals' mind full-time. Why? Since they can scrap that metal.

Simply remember that the more significant metals are aluminium and copper

67. Web Security Specialist:

Security is a significant worry for organizations and people.

Other than mastery and some showcasing, it doesn't cost a lot to begin a business ensuring others' equipment and programming.

68. Freelance Barkeep:

If you can make a mean Manhattan, Cosmopolitan and other oft-requested beverages, take a stab at showcasing yourself as an independent barkeep for private gatherings and occasions.

69. Training Dogs:

Imagine yourself been the next Cesar Millan? This is another easy business idea with the potential for high benefits.

70. Referral Administration:

Regardless of whether another business or family simply moved into town, you can elude them to the correct sellers, sitters or eateries. Your solitary expense would system and promoting yourself to the network.

71. Packing Service:

Nobody loves the idea of packing up loads themselves. That is the reason they'll recruit others to pack and burden their assets up. You truly don't have to buy anything without repayment, since boxes and tape will be remembered for your last cost.

You'll most likely despite everything be a less expensive alternative than proficient movers.

72. Composing as Well as Recording a Melody:

In the event that you have the melodic cleaves, you can make a vocation out of composing your own music. What's more is that, it doesn't need to be the most recent of

Taylor Swift single - you could compose jingles for webcasts or nearby organizations.

73. Concert and Show Promotion:

if you have some skills with promotion and are enthusiastic about getting the message out about upcoming occasions, at this point you can begin working with specialists, scenes and labels to produce buzz with basically no speculation on your part.

74. Analyzer or Analyst:

Organizations are regularly searching for people to test and survey their items. You can likewise begin your own blog where you audit items in a specific specialty.

75. Fashion Design:

Locales like Etsy now make it possible for you to sell your one of a kind style structures. Regardless of whether you're not into high style, you can begin making your own T-shirts and produce through locales like CafePress.

76. **Importing Items:**

You can buy items from abroad in mass and begin selling them at a markup. That is the means by which Pura Vida began.

77. **Make-Up Artist:** Regardless of whether if it's for an uncommon event like a wedding or for Halloween, individuals frequently pay a huge sum for experts to do their cosmetics.

78. **Hairdresser:**

In case you're exceptional on the present styles and can trim hair, at this point you can begin your own salon from your home.

79. **Selling Snacks and Drinks:**

Have you at any point left a game or show parched and starving? We've all been there. That is the reason you see individuals selling jugs of water and hotdog after an occasion.

Unlike putting resources into a food truck or truck, you can begin with only a cooler.

80. **Voice-Over Craftsman:**

Since organizations are making their own content, for example, recordings and web recordings, they're searching for brilliant voices.

On the off chance that this is something you can probably do without stress, at this point you could transform it into a worthwhile profession.

81. **Brewer:**

You can purchase a lager kit for under $100 and begin tinkering around with blending your own brew.

82. **Wine Making:**

You needn't bother with a vineyard to begin making wine. You can begin by developing your very own portion grapes or buying juice.

In the event that your little cluster of wine ends up well and you begin making some money, you could in the long run start your own vineyard or winery.

83. **Selling Eggs:**

Ranch new eggs are a major business at the present time. You can get in on the activity by buying a few hens and building your own chicken coop.

84. **Homemade Bakery:**

The size of the market for home-prepared bread may astound you. You should give this a try.

85. **Creating Customized Care Bundles:**

Numerous individuals appreciate customize care bundles that they can give out as gifts.

To start, you have to discover a specialty, similar to occasion bundles, and begin filling each with treats.

86. Educator:

You can sell exercises instructing individuals on how to play an instrument, cook a feast or even work out.

You basically simply need your own insight and promoting to begin.

87. Airbnb Host:

On the off chance that you have an additional room or home, consider leasing it out on Airbnb as opposed to letting it stay there empty.

88. Property Management:

Proprietors can't generally monitor their properties or keep up them by means of cleaning and cutting.

A property management organization deals with these errands for occupied landowners.

89. Laundry and Dry-Cleaning Services:

Nearly everybody has garments that should be cleaned or pressed, and in many cases, they don't have the tolerance or time to deal with these errands all alone.

That is the reason numerous individuals pay others to do it for them.

90. Clothing Alteration Administration:

On the off chance that you realize how to sew or supplant fastens or zippers, at this point you have another business idea for individuals who can't leave behind their preferred garments.

It's additionally economical to dispatch this sort of business.

91. Web Based Dating Specialist:

An ever increasing number of individuals are going to a web based dating to discover a match, however it tends to be overpowering when simply beginning.

In the event that you have experience with the zone, at that point a few people are eager to pay for exhortation.

92. Sourcing Administration:

You can discover items or administrations for nearby organizations and exchange them at a markup.

93. Travel Organization:

Despite the fact that there are several movement sites out there, a great number of people don't have the opportunity or persistence to think about the costs of flights and lodging rates. That is the reason there's as yet a requirement for individuals to do the legwork for them

94. Toy Production:

Regardless of whether it's cutting a doll out of wood or utilizing a 3D printer, making toys can be a worthwhile business thought.

95. Food Conveyance Service:

A few people feel they can't leave the workplace to get food, and others would prefer not to leave their homes. That is the point at which they'll get in touch with you to get and convey food to their destinations.

96. Perfume Making:

Everyone desires to smell good and the art of home-made perfume can be practiced by anyone and could be sold to friends, neighbours and colleagues.

97. Direct Sales Representative:

Being a neighbourhood salesperson for organizations like Avon, Mary Kay, and Pampered Chef expects you to get the message out about their items by facilitating a gathering or selling them on the web.

Most starter packs cost around $100 and furnish you with all that you have to turn into an agent.

98. Consultation:

With professional knowledge and access to information or are you an expert in a particular field?

Make it generate money for you by offering legitimate guidance to individuals as well as businesses on the best possible ways, methods to apply in order to achieve their goals as well as objectives of an organisation when dealing with a firm.

The primary costs includes an office space, office desk and chairs, create a website, business cards, fliers e.t.c . Need more help? Look up a model counselling guide.

99. Auto Repair/ Detailing:

If you have a carport, with some devices and information, you can start your own auto mechanics shop.

With the available carport space, you could establish a portable auto fix business where you go to the stalled vehicle. If you like working with vehicles yet you are definitely not a technician, at that point think about washing and enumerating vehicles.

100. **Tour Guide:**

Individuals who are knowledgeable about places, destinations, historic sites could be become guides to tourist and make a living from it.

CONCLUSION

The above list of business ideas are great side hustles you can start up with $100 or less and make a substantial cash flow with little monetary investment. With full commitment and diligence to the above businesses, you can earn a whole lot with less than a $100. Give it a go!

Made in the USA
Columbia, SC
31 May 2023

17553527R00024